A Fleet in Being

Shilka Publishing
Apt 2049
Chynoweth House
Trevissome Park
Truro
TR4 8UN

www.shilka.co.uk

Ordering Information:

Quantity sales. Special discounts are available on quantity purchases by corporations, associations, and others. For details, contact the "Special Sales Department" at the address above.

A Fleet in Being/ Russell Phillips. —2nd ed.

ISBN 978-0-9927648-0-7

A Fleet in Being

Austro-Hungarian Warships of WWI

Russell Phillips

Contents

Contents

Introduction

From 1904 to 1913, Admiral Graf Rudolf Montecuccoli was Commander in Chief of the Austro-Hungarian Kaiserliche und Königliche Kriegsmarine (Imperial and Royal War Fleet). Montecuccoli was a driving force behind the modernisation of the fleet, in which he was helped by support from Archduke Franz Ferdinand. He was succeeded in 1913 by Admiral Anton Haus, who became the only active duty officer not a member of the Imperial house to be given the rank of Grand Admiral, in 1916. He died of pneumonia in February 1917 and was succeeded as commander in chief by Admiral Maximilian Njegovan. After the mutiny at Cattaro, Njegovan was retired on the 1st of March 1918, replaced by Rear Admiral Miklós Horthy.

The navy's main ports were Pola, Trieste, and Cattaro, while the Naval Academy was in Fiume. The navy's ships were supplied primarily by Stabilimento Tecnico Triestino (STT) in Trieste, Cantiere Navale Triestino (CNT) in Monfalcone, Whitehead in Fiume, and Danubius (a company set up and subsidised by the Hungarian government) also based in Fiume.

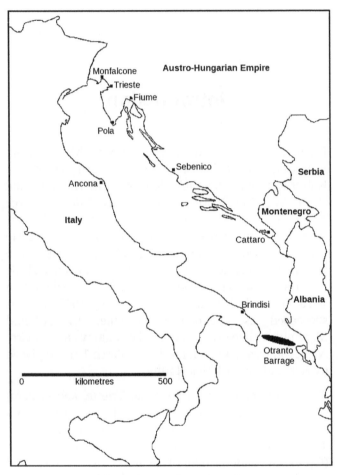

The Adriatic during WWI

Unique Difficulties

The Austro-Hungarian navy faced some unique difficulties. Although one of Europe's great powers, Austria-Hungary was not a colonial power, and so did not feel the need for a large, powerful navy. Since range was not of great importance, and finances were often tight, Austro-Hungarian warships were generally smaller than their counterparts in other navies.

The Dual Monarchy's system of government exacerbated the problems of naval funding. The Austro-Hungarian Compromise of 1867 meant that both Austrian and Hungarian parliaments had to agree naval budgets. Hungary, not having a coastline, generally preferred to spend money on the army rather than the navy. The Hungarian parliament would sometimes block funding of naval projects altogether, or make approval contingent upon certain concessions. Archduke Franz Ferdinand was a keen supporter of the navy, however, and campaigned energetically on its behalf. After he and his wife were assassinated in 1914, they were laid in state aboard SMS *Viribus Unitis*.

The navy drew sailors from all parts of the dual monarchy, which led to problems with communication, since the empire had eleven official languages. All sailors had to learn some essential commands in German, but officers had to be able to speak at least four of the empire's languages. Different nationalities tended to gravitate towards particular roles: Germans and Czechs were often engineers or signalmen, many gunners were Hungarian, stokers were Croats, and deck crews were frequently Italian.

Naval Aviation

The Austro-Hungarian navy saw the potential of aircraft as early as 1910, and started to develop seaplanes for both reconnaissance and attack missions. Given the problems that the navy had always faced with funding, senior naval officers were quick to see that relatively cheap aircraft could be fitted with anti-ship weapons such as torpedoes. Naval aviation was based at Pola and operated over land as well as over the Adriatic. Like the surface fleet, the air arm tied up numbers of Allied aircraft out of all proportion to its own strength. Two Austro-Hungarian naval aircraft, the Lohner flying boats L 132 and L 135, were the first aircraft to sink an enemy submarine, when they bombed the French submarine *Foucault* in September 1916. After sinking her, they took her crew on board until a torpedo boat arrived to take them away.

War Service

The Austro-Hungarian navy functioned largely as a "fleet in being" during World War 1, with its capital ships spending much of the war in port. This policy was partly due to a lack of coal and fear of mines in the Adriatic, though it seems likely that the superior strength which the Allies could bring to bear was also a factor. Although Austria-Hungary's fleet was not large, it did force the Allies to keep a significant force in the Mediterranean, to counter any possibility of the fleet making a major sortie. Consequently, the Italian navy and most of the French navy were kept in the area, along with some British units. Had the Austro-Hungarian fleet committed to a major battle, it would likely have suffered significant losses, allowing the Allies to reduce their presence in the area.

Immediately after Italy's declaration of war in 1915, the Austro-Hungarian fleet sailed to conduct shore bombardment operations against the eastern Italian coast. The three Allied navies faced difficulties co-ordinating with each other, which made them less effective than would otherwise be expected. Consequently, Austro-Hungarian and German submarines were able to operate far more effectively than would have been the case had they faced a well-organised opponent.

When the German cruisers SMS *Goeben* and SMS *Breslau* left Messina, Italy, heading for Istanbul on the 7th of August 1914, the Germans asked their Austro-Hungarian allies for support. The Austro-Hungarian fleet was not yet fully mobilised, but the Tegetthoffs and Radetzkys were available, as were some smaller ships. The Austro-Hungarian high command was wary of provoking Great Britain, with whom they were not yet at war, and so the fleet sailed, but went no further south than Brindisi.

Otranto Barrage

In late 1915, the Allies set up the Otranto Barrage, an attempt to blockade the Otranto Straits between Brindisi and Corfu. Initially, the barrage was manned by a force of 60 armed trawlers, with 20 on station at any one time, supported by aircraft and destroyers. The trawlers were equipped with light steel nets known as indicator nets, which were intended to alert the surface ships to passing submarines. The barrage only caught a single submarine - the U6, in 1916.

A number of night-time raids were mounted against the barrage, usually on nights with a full moon. Five raids were carried out in 1915, nine in 1916, ten in 1917, and one in 1918. A second, large attack was planned in 1918 but was called off (see the *Tegetthoff*-class entry for details).

Battle of the Otranto Straits

The most successful raid was carried out on the night of the 14/15th of May, 1917. Three cruisers (SMS *Novara, Helgoland, Saida*), two destroyers (*Csepel, Balaton*) and three submarines (U-4, U-27, German UC-25) sank 14 trawlers and damaged four more. In many cases, the Austro-Hungarians gave the trawler crews a warning and time to abandon ship before opening fire, though some trawler crews decided to fight instead. The captain of the trawler *Gowan Lee* was awarded the Victoria Cross for his part in the battle.

At 07:00 the Italian flotilla leader *Mirabello*, with the French destroyers *Commandant Rivière, Bisson*, and *Cimeterre* intercepted the main Austro-Hungarian force, but being out-gunned, chose to shadow rather than engage. At 07:45, two British cruisers (HMS *Dartmouth* and *Bristol*) and five Italian destroyers engaged the destroyers *Csepel* and *Balaton*, which had been conducting a diversionary attack off the Albanian coast. After a short fight, in which one Italian destroyer's boilers were disabled, the Allies retreated as they came into range of the coastal batteries at Durazzo.

At 09:00 HMS *Bristol* sighted the Austrian cruisers, and the Allied force turned to engage. Some of the Allied destroyers started to suffer from mechanical problems; those that did not were tasked with protecting those that did, so that the two cruisers continued the battle without the destroyers. Meanwhile, reinforcements from both sides were dispatched. By 11:00, the Austro-Hungarian cruiser *Novara* had been crippled, but *Sankt Georg* was approaching with a force of destroyers and torpedo boats. Acton, the Allied commander, temporarily withdrew to consolidate his forces, allowing the Austro-Hungarians to take *Novara* under tow.

Acton broke off the pursuit, though an Italian destroyer misread the signal and attempted to launch a torpedo attack. It was driven off by heavy gunfire. SMS *Csepel* and *Balaton* rejoined the others, and the Austro-Hungarian surface force returned to Cattaro. The German UC-25 later caused serious damage to HMS *Dartmouth* with a torpedo attack, and the French destroyer *Boutefeu* was sunk by a mine whilst pursuing UC-25.

Cattaro Mutiny

As the war went on, some sailors became disaffected. Influenced by the Russian revolution in 1917 and strikes in Vienna, sailors in Cattaro mutinied on the 1st of February, 1918. A red flag (one of the official signal flags) was raised on *Sankt Georg* as a signal to the other ships in the port that the mutiny had begun. Mutineers took control of many of the ships in the base, raising red flags, which became a symbol of the mutiny. Some ships remained under orders but raised the red flag in order to avoid being fired upon by the larger ships. The mutineers made some attempt to spread the mutiny to other units, but these appear to have been prevented by telegraphists discreetly limiting the range of the transmitting equipment.

In the evening, a list of demands were handed to Kontreadmiral Hansa. The demands included immediate steps to arrange a general peace, complete independence from Germany, a democratic form of government and better treatment for sailors, with less differential between the treatment of sailors and officers. The local army commander drew up plans to stop the mutiny by force, including the use of artillery against the ships, but Admiral Hansa hoped to negotiate an end to the affair.

On the 2nd of February, the army gave an ultimatum to the sailors, giving them three hours to return to order. Hansa had this extended by two hours, on condition that the ships make no movement or aggressive action. The cruisers SMS *Helgoland* and *Novara*, along with some torpedo boats, were still under orders. They managed to make steam and move out of the reach of the mutineers' guns, making signals that they were moving out of range of the shore batteries. Once they were clear, they struck the red flag and raised the imperial ensign. The captain of the German submarine station put his submarines under the disposal of Linienschiffskapitän Heyssler on SMS *Helgoland*, but Heyssler was not prepared to torpedo valuable ships.

The Third Battleship Division, consisting of the three *Erzherzog Karl*-class pre-dreadnoughts, had sailed from Pola for Cattaro. A deadline had been given to the mutineers of 10:00 on the 3rd of February, after which time, if they had not returned to orders, the mutiny would be put down by force. The leaders of the mutiny were determined to carry it through, but after a brief fight, during which some shells were fired from shore artillery, some of the petty officers and sailors helped their officers take control, and the mutiny was over.

Around 800 men were arrested, 40 of whom were put on trial. Judgements were issued, and sentences handed down, on the 10th of February. Four men were sentenced to death, the sentence being carried out the next day. Charges were later brought against another 392 men, though the charges against 348 of them were later dropped.

After the War

Not wishing to hand the navy over to the Allies, in late 1918 the Emperor gave the entire Austro-Hungarian Navy and merchant fleet, including all harbours, arsenals, and shore fortifications, to the National Council of the newly-formed Kingdom of Serbs, Croats, and Slovenes. This transfer was ignored by the Allies in the subsequent peace treaty, and all the ships were transferred to various Allied nations as war reparations.

Dreadnought Battleships

As the Italians planned to start construction of their first dreadnought, in 1908 Admiral Montecuccoli announced a new generation of battleships of around 18,000-19,000 tons displacement. The basic design of what was to become the *Tegetthoff* class was accepted in April 1909. STT needed work for their skilled workers if they were to retain them, and Montecuccoli suggested that they start work at their own risk until the naval budget was approved. The risk was believed to be minimal, especially as Italy had by now started work on her first dreadnought.

However, funding for the new class of ships was initially refused, on the grounds that the army needed the money to administer the newly-annexed Bosnia and Herzegovina. Construction continued when Montecuccoli personally guaranteed a 32 million Kronen credit. Funding was eventually obtained, but with the condition that the fourth ship of the class be built by the Hungarian company Danubius. Danubius had no experience with large ship construction and so *Szent István* cost more and took longer to complete than the other three ships of the *Tegetthoff* class.

Tegetthoff Class

Tegetthoff, Viribus Unitis, Prinz Eugen, Szent István

SMS *Tegetthoff*

Tegetthoff, Viribus Unitis, and *Prinz Eugen* bombarded the naval base at Ancona and the coast of Montenegro in 1915. *Szent István* was not completed in time to take part in this action, which was the only time the class fired their guns in anger.

In 1918, Admiral Horthy, the navy's new commander in chief, planned to carry out a raid on the Otranto Barrage in conjunction with an army offensive in northern Italy. As *Tegetthoff* and *Szent István* sailed south, they were spotted by Italian MAS boats, which intercepted and attacked. *Szent István* was hit amidships by two torpedoes. She began to list, and after about two and a half hours she capsized. On hearing the news of *Szent István*'s loss, Admiral Horthy aborted the mission, assuming that it had been compromised.

Displacement: 20,014 tonnes

Dimensions: 152.2m x 27.3m x 8.9m

Machinery: 4 turbines, 12 boilers, 27,000 shp

Speed: 20.3 knots

Complement: 1,087

Armour:

Belt 150-280mm

Deck 30-48mm

Slopes 48mm

Torpedo bulkhead 50mm

Main turrets 60-280mm

Casemates 180mm

Conning tower 60-280mm

Armament:

12x 30.5cm L/45 guns

12x 15cm L/50 guns

14x 66mm L/50 quick-firing guns

4x 66mm L/50 quick-firing AA guns

2x 66mm L/18 landing guns

4x 53.3cm torpedo tubes

Ersatz Monarch (Improved *Tegetthoff*) Class

Commonly referred to as the "Ersatz Monarch" class after the contract name for the first vessel, this class was never officially named. In April 1911, when the triple turrets for the *Tegetthoffs* were close to completion, Skoda submitted plans to the Naval Section of the War Ministry for turrets mounting two or three 34.5cm guns. They proposed that the twin turrets could be superimposed on the triple turrets, and fitted on the centreline. The Naval Section rejected these designs, and ordered preparatory designs of their own, which would cut down weight while maximising firepower and protection by sacrificing range, since they were only ever likely to fight in the Adriatic and Mediterranean.

In December 1911, 26 designs were submitted to the Naval Section from various private companies, but all were rejected. Skoda, meanwhile, were asked to work out new turret designs, and the gun calibre was increased slightly to 35cm. The final ship design was presented in July 1914, with the details given below.

Like the *Tegetthoff* class, there were issues regarding funding. Admiral Haus, the naval C-in-C, wanted to order the new ships in March 1913, as the STT yard urgently needed new orders. The Hungarian parliament blocked the order, arguing that ordering construction on credit would be illegal, and that funds would have to wait for the 1914/1915 budget. STT and Danubius were ordered to build two of the dreadnoughts in June 1914, but the outbreak of war meant that the keels were never laid down.

Pre-Dreadnought Battleships

Monarch Class

Monarch, Budapest, Wien

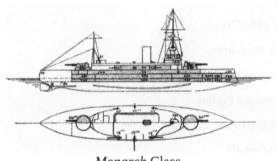

Monarch Class

The *Monarch*-class battleships were built at the end of the 19th century. All three ships had 12 boilers, producing 8,500hp in *Monarch* and *Wien*, giving a top speed of 15.5 knots. *Budapest* had more modern engines, producing 9,180hp and giving a top speed of 17.5 knots.

They saw little service during the war, but *Budapest* and *Wien* bombarded Italian positions in 1915 and 1917.

Wien was sunk by Italian MAS boats while in harbour at Trieste in 1917. The other two ships survived the war and were assigned to Great Britain as war reparations.

Displacement: 5,547 tonnes

Dimensions: 99.22m x 17m x 6.4m

Machinery: 12 boilers, 8,500 hp (*Budapest*: 9,180 hp)

Speed: 15.5 knots (*Budapest*: 17.5 knots)

Complement: 469

Armour:

Belt 220-270mm

Deck 40-60mm

Main turrets 250mm

Casemates 80mm

Conning tower 220mm

Armament:

4x 24cm L/40 guns

6x 15cm L/40 guns

1x 66mm AA gun

12x 47mm L/33 guns

2x 45cm torpedo tubes

Habsburg Class

Habsburg, Árpád, Babenburg

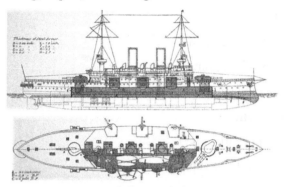

Habsburg Class

The *Habsburg* class of three sea-going battleships was launched in the early years of the twentieth century. They saw little service in the war, though *Árpád* and *Babenburg* bombarded Ancona in 1915. In 1916, they were decommissioned, and assigned to Great Britain at the end of the war.

Displacement: 8,232 tonnes

Dimensions: 114.6m x 19.8m x 7.5m

Machinery: 16 boilers, 15,000 ihp

Speed: 19 knots

Complement: 638

Armour:

Belt 180-220mm

Deck 40mm

Main turrets 280mm

Casemates 210mm

Conning tower 150mm

Armament:

3x 24cm L/40 guns

12x 15cm L/40 guns

10x 66mm L/45 guns

6x 47mm L/44 quick-firing guns

2x 47mm L/33 quick-firing guns

2x 45cm torpedo tubes

Erzherzog Karl Class

Erzherzog Karl, Erzherzog Friedrich, Erzherzog Ferdinand Max

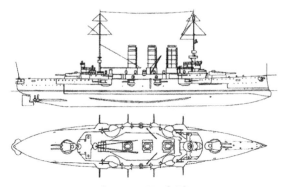

Erzherzog Karl Class

The *Erzherzog Karl* class were built at Trieste between 1902 and 1905. They were of reasonably modern design at the time they were built, though like many Austrian ships, they were relatively small. They saw little action, but did bombard Ancona in May 1915, and helped suppress a mutiny in Cattaro in February 1918. All three ships were to take part in the planned attack on the Otranto Barrage in June 1918, but returned to port with the rest of the Austro-Hungarian force after *Szent István* was sunk.

During the war, two of the 66mm guns were fitted into anti-aircraft mountings.

Erzherzog Karl and *Erzherzog Friedrich* were ceded to France, and *Erzherzog Ferdinand Max* to Great Britain as war reparations.

Displacement: 10,472 tonnes

Dimensions: 126.2m x 21.8m x 7.5m

Machinery: 12 boilers, 18,000 ihp

Speed: 20.5 knots

Complement: 700

Armour:

Belt 210mm

Deck 55mm

Main turrets 240mm

Casemates 150mm

Conning tower 220mm

Armament:

4x 24cm L/40 guns

12x 19cm L/42 guns

12x 66mm L/45 guns

4x 47mm L/44 quick-firing guns

2x 47mm L/33 quick-firing guns

4x 37mm guns

2x 45cm torpedo tubes

Radetzky Class

Radetzky, Erzherzog Franz Ferdinand, Zrinyi

SMS *Radetzky*

The *Radetzky* class were built between 1907 and 1910 by STT in Trieste. The 30.5cm guns and 24cm guns were mounted in twin turrets. In October 1914, *Radetzky* bombarded French shore batteries that were shelling the naval base at Cattaro. In 1915 all three ships carried out shore bombardments against Italy. They saw little service during the rest of the war.

In November 1918, *Radetzky* and *Zrinyi* sailed out of Pola, crewed by Yugoslav crews. They flew American flags in order to avoid the Italian fleet and surrendered to American forces. American officers inspected the ships with interest, and were impressed by the cleanliness displayed on deck. They were less impressed with the accommodation arrangements. Officers were housed in considerable comfort, but the crew quarters were cramped, dark, and stuffy.

All three ships passed to Italy after the war.

Displacement: 14,508 tonnes

Dimensions: 137.5m x 24.6m x 8.1m

Machinery: 12 boilers, 19,800 ihp

Speed: 20.5 knots

Complement: 890

Armour:

Belt 100-230mm

Deck 48mm

Slopes 48mm

Torpedo bulkhead 54mm

Main turrets 60-250mm

Armament:

4x 30.5cm L/45 guns

8x 24cm L/45 guns

20x 10cm L/50 guns

6x 66mm L/45 quick-firing guns (used as AA guns)

2x 66mm L/18 landing guns

4x 47mm L/44 quick-firing guns

1x 47mm L/33 quick-firing guns

3x 45cm torpedo tubes

Cruisers

Austria-Hungary's cruisers led several raids against the Otranto Barrage. The modified *Admiral Spauns*, in particular, led destroyers and torpedo boats in several raids against the barrage in 1915, 1916 and 1917. They were also to take part in the raid that was intended to take place in 1918, but which was called off after *Szent István* was sunk.

Kaiser Franz Josef I Class

Kaiser Franz Josef I, Kaiserin Elisabeth

SMS *Kaiserin Elisabeth*

This class was a compromise brought about by limits on funding. They were heavily armed and armoured for their size (when built, they each had two 24cm and six 15cm guns), and so were somewhat reminiscent of the "pocket battleship" concept that the Germans adopted in the 1930s. The class was obsolete by 1914.

Kaiser Franz Joseph I was involved in shore bombardment operations in 1914 and 1916, before being assigned to local defence service at Cattaro. In 1917, she was disarmed and became a floating headquarters. After the war, she was assigned to France as war reparations, but, overloaded with machinery, she sank in a gale while transiting to France.

Kaiserin Elisabeth was stationed in China at the outbreak of war. She took part in the defence of the German naval base at Tsingtao when it was besieged by Japanese and British forces. Her 15cm and 4.7cm guns were removed during the siege, to become the "Batterie Elisabeth", and she was scuttled before the fortress surrendered.

Displacement: 3,967 tonnes

Dimensions: 102.6m x 14.7m x 5.7m

Machinery: Eight boilers, 8,450 ihp

Speed: 19 knots

Complement: 450

Armament:

8x 15cm guns

16x 47mm quick-firing guns

1x machine gun

4x 36cm torpedo tubes

Kaiserin und Königin Maria Theresia Class

Kaiserin und Königin Maria Theresia

SMS *Kaiserin und Königin Maria Theresia*

Kaiserin und Königin Maria Theresia saw service as a harbour guard ship until 1916. She was disarmed and decommissioned in 1917, and served as an accommodation vessel for German submarine crews.

Displacement: 5,330 tonnes

Dimensions: 111.7m x 16.3m x 6.1m

Machinery: Four boilers, 9,000 hp

Speed: 18.9 knots

Complement: 475

Armour:

Belt 100mm

Deck 38-57mm

Barbettes 100mm

Casemates 80mm

Conning Tower 20-50mm

Armament:

2x 19cm guns

8x 15cm guns

14x 47mm quick-firing guns

4x 37mm revolving guns

2x 66mm landing guns

4x 45cm torpedo tubes

Kaiser Karl VI Class

Kaiser Karl VI

SMS *Kaiser Karl VI*

Launched in 1898 and commissioned in 1900, she saw some action during the war, including several shore bombardment missions. In February 1918, the crew took part in the mutiny at Cattaro. After the mutiny had been put down, she was moved to Sebenico. She was ceded to Great Britain as war reparations in 1920.

Displacement: 6,166 tonnes

Dimensions: 117.9m x 17.3m x 6.3m

Machinery: 16 boilers, 12,900 hp

Speed: 20.8 knots

Complement: 570

Armour:

Belt 180-220mm

Deck 32-64mm

Barbettes 205mm

Casemates 75mm

Armament:

2x 24cm L/40 guns

8x 15cm L/40 guns

16x 47mm L/44 guns

2x 47mm L/33 (replaced by a single 66mm L/50 AA gun in June 1917)

2x 45cm torpedo tubes

Sankt Georg Class

Sankt Georg

Funding for the construction of *Sankt Georg* was approved in 1900. She was laid down the following year, launched in 1903 and commissioned in 1905.

She saw some action during the war, including several shore bombardment missions in 1915 and 1916. In February 1918, the ship's crew initiated the mutiny at Cattaro. After the mutiny had been put down, she was moved to Teodo.

After the war, she was ceded to Great Britain as war reparations.

Displacement: 7,289 tonnes

Dimensions: 123.2m x 19m x 6.8m

Machinery: 16 boilers, 15,000 ihp

Speed: 22 knots

Complement: 630

Armour:

Belt 165-210mm

Deck 36-60mm

Barbettes 210mm

Casemates 150mm

Conning tower 125-200mm

Armament:

2x 24cm L/40 guns

5x 19cm L/42 guns

4x 15cm L/40 guns

9x 66mm L/45 guns

8x 4.7cm L/45 quick-firing guns

1x 66mm AA gun (added in 1916)

2x 45cm torpedo tubes

Zenta Class

Zenta, Aspern, Szigetvár

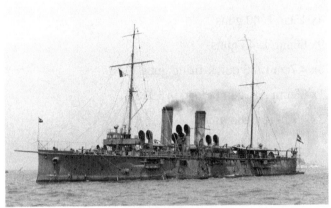

SMS *Aspern*

The *Zenta*-class cruisers were obsolete by 1914, but all three saw active service. *Zenta* was sunk in 1914, the others were disarmed in 1918 and served briefly as accommodation vessels. They were allocated to Great Britain after the war, and sold to Italy for scrap.

Displacement: 2,313 tonnes

Dimensions: 96.9m x 10.5m x 4.2m

Machinery: 8 boilers, 7,800 hp

Speed: 20 knots

Complement: 308

Armour:

Belt 25mm

Conning Tower 25mm

Casemates 35mm

Deck 50mm

Armament:

8x 12cm guns

8x 47mm guns

2x machine guns

2x 45cm torpedo tubes

Admiral Spaun Class

Admiral Spaun

SMS *Admiral Spaun*

The design of *Admiral Spaun* sacrificed armament for speed and armour protection, the intention being to use hit-and-run tactics. Her propulsion system had many problems, preventing her from taking part in major actions. There were plans to upgrade her armament later in the war, but these plans never came to fruition.

Displacement: 3,500 tonnes

Dimensions: 130.6m x 12.8m x 5.3m

Machinery: Six turbines, 16 boilers, 25,130 shp

Speed: 27.1 knots

Complement: 327

Armour:

Side 60mm

Deck 20mm

Conning Tower 50mm

Armament:

7x 10cm guns

1x 47mm landing gun

2x 45cm torpedo tubes (added in 1916)

1x machine gun

Modified Admiral Spaun Class

Saida, Helgoland, Novara

SMS *Saida*

Newer turbines were used in these ships, which weighed 52 tonnes less than those in the *Admiral Spaun*. The weight saving was used to strengthen the ship and improve the armament.

Political considerations led to *Helgoland* and *Novara* being built in the Hungarian shipyard of Danubius, in Fiume.

All three saw extensive service during the war, *Novara* being badly damaged during the Battle of the Otranto Straits. Plans were drawn up to increase their armament towards the end of the war, though these plans were never acted upon.

Displacement: 3,500 tonnes

Dimensions: 130.6m x 12.8m x 5.3m

Machinery: Six turbines, 16 boilers, 30,178 shp

Speed: 27 knots

Complement: 340

Armour:

Side 60mm

Deck 20mm

Turrets 8-40mm

Conning Tower 50mm

Armament:

9x 10cm guns

1x 66mm AA gun (added in 1917)

1x 47mm landing gun

6x 45cm torpedo tubes (added in 1917)

Ex-Chinese Cruiser Class

China ordered four light cruisers in 1913, but work was still at an early stage when the shipyards were overrun by the Italians. In 1917, Austro-Hungarian troops recaptured the area, and found that the cruisers had not suffered much damage. It was decided to continue work on the large cruiser, with a proposed configuration as detailed below, but work had not been restarted by the time the war ended.

Armament:

8x 15cm guns

9x 90mm AA guns

4x 45cm torpedo tubes

Ersatz Zenta Class

Three fast light cruisers as detailed below were included in the 1914/1915 naval budget, but when war broke out, they still had not been laid down. In 1915 the design was changed as follows: armament became two 19cm and six 15cm guns, four 90mm AA guns and two torpedo tubes, and belt armour was increased to 120-150mm. No work was carried out, however, and the redesign owed as much to wishful thinking as anything else.

Displacement: 4,950 tonnes

Dimensions: 153.1m x 13.7m x 6.4m

Machinery: Turbines and boilers, 38,000 shp

Speed: 30.1 knots

Armour:

Side 20mm

Belt 38mm

Armament:

14x 12cm guns

1x 47mm gun

1x 66mm landing gun

2x 45cm torpedo tubes

Panter Class

Panter, Leopard

Launched in 1885 and built in Great Britain, both *Panter* (Panther) class vessels had their main armament removed in 1909/1910. They were obsolete by 1914. *Leopard* was used as a harbour defence ship at Pola, while *Panter* was attached to the submarine commanders' school.

Displacement: 1,557 tonnes

Dimensions: 69m x 10m x 4.3m

Machinery: 6,000 hp

Speed: 18 knots

Complement: 202

Armour:

Deck 50mm

Armament:

4x 9 pounder

10x 3 pounder

4x 35cm torpedo tubes

Destroyers and Torpedo Boats

In 1904, when the *Huszár* class was introduced, 200 tons was considered a good size for a destroyer. By 1910, however, displacement had doubled due to the use of turbine propulsion. In 1913, all torpedo boats were ordered to be given numbers instead of names, initially with a letter suffix to indicate where they were built (E: England, F: Fiume, M: Monfalcone, T: Trieste). The suffix letter was dropped in 1917.

Had the empire survived the war, plans in the naval budget would have seen a new 2,400-ton flotilla leader, 1,000 ton destroyer, and all the existing torpedo boats converted to minesweepers. The duties of the torpedo boats were to be taken over by even smaller MTBs and MGBs.

Huszár Class

Huszár, Ulan, Streiter, Wildfang, Scharfschutze, Uskoke, Turul, Pandur, Csikós, Reka, Dinara, Velebit

A prototype 400-ton destroyer was built for the Austro-Hungarian navy by Yarrow in 1904, with more built to the same design at domestic shipyards. They were up-gunned to the configuration detailed here in 1912, but were still considered obsolete by the time war broke out.

Displacement: 389.4 tonnes

Dimensions: 68.4m x 6.3m x 1.9m

Machinery: Four boilers, 6,000 ihp

Speed: 28.4 knots

Complement: 70

Armament:

7x 66mm gun

2x 45cm torpedo tubes

Tátra Class

Tátra, Balaton, Csepel, Liua, Triglav, Orjen

Four shipyards tendered for the construction of six 800-ton destroyers in 1910. The Danubius yard was awarded the contract, at least partly for political reasons (to try and ensure that the Hungarians would not block the following year's naval budget). *Liua* and *Triglav* were sunk by mines in 1915; the other four were ceded to Italy in 1920.

Displacement: 850 tonnes

Dimensions: 83.5m x 7.8m x 3.0m

Machinery: Six boilers, 20,640 shp

Speed: 32.6 knots

Complement: 105

Armament:

2x 10cm guns

6x 66mm guns

4x 45cm torpedo tubes

Ersatz Tátra Class

Triglav, Lika, Dukla, Uzsok

Six extra *Tátra*-class destroyers were authorised in 1914, but never started. This class of four was authorised in 1916 in order to replace losses, and all were launched in 1917. After the war, three were ceded to Italy and the other to France.

Displacement: 880 tonnes

Dimensions: 85.4m x 7.8m x 2.4m

Machinery: Six boilers, 22,360 shp

Speed: 32.6 knots

Complement: 114

Armament:

2x 10cm guns

6x 66mm guns (2 on AA mounts)

4x 45cm torpedo tubes

1x machine gun

Improved Tátra Class

Four up-gunned Ersatz Tátra destroyers were ordered in 1917, but were never laid down due to shortages of steel.

Displacement: 880 tonnes

Dimensions: 85.4m x 7.8m x 2.4m

Machinery: Six boilers, 22,360 shp

Speed: 32.6 knots

Armament:

2x 12cm guns

2x 90mm AA guns

4x 45cm torpedo tubes

Warasdiner Class

Warasdiner

Launched in 1912 as the *Lung Tuan* and intended for sale to China, she was taken over by the Austro-Hungarian navy in 1914, renamed and rearmed.

Displacement: 389.4 tonnes

Dimensions: 68.4m x 6.3m x 1.9m

Machinery: Four boilers, 6,000 ihp

Speed: 30 knots

Complement: 75

Armament:

6x 66mm guns

4x 45cm torpedo tubes

Tb1 T Class

Tb1-6 T

Originally there were to be eight of these boats, all built at Trieste. However, due to internal politics, only six were built at Trieste, with more being built at Fiume (see the entry for the Tb7 class) During the war, these boats performed escort, minesweeping and anti-submarine work. All were allocated to Italy in 1920.

Displacement: 116 tonnes

Dimensions: 44.2m x 4.3m x 1.2m

Machinery: Two oil-fired boilers, 1,500 ihp

Speed: 28 knots

Complement: 20

Armament:

2x 47mm guns

2x 45cm torpedo tubes

Tb7 F Class

Tb7-12 F

These boats were built by Danubius at Fiume. Danubius had less experience with this type of boat, but was selected to build these vessels after intervention by the Hungarian parliament. The crew of Tb11 F mutinied in October 1917 and deserted to Italy. All the boats survived the war and were allocated to Italy in 1920.

Displacement: 131.5 tonnes

Dimensions: 44.2m x 4.3m x 1.5m

Machinery: Two oil-fired boilers, 2,400 ihp

Speed: 26.5 knots

Complement: 20

Armament:

2x 47mm guns

2x 45cm torpedo tubes

Tb17 E Class

Tb17 E

Displacement: 124 tonnes

Dimensions: 45m x 4.5 x 2.3m

Machinery: 1,900 ihp

Speed: 25 knots

Complement: 21

Armament:

2x 47mm quick-firing guns

3x torpedo tubes

Tb50 torpedo boats at Pola

Tb50 Class

Tb50 E, Tb51-63 T, Tb64-73 F

The lead boat of the class was built in Yarrow, and British plans and engineering assistance were used in the construction of the rest of the class, built at Trieste and Fiume. All members of the class saw active service and survived the war, though some were damaged.

Displacement: 210 tonnes

Dimensions: 56.9m x 5.4m x 1.4m

Machinery: Two boilers, 3,000 ihp

Speed: 26.2 knots

Complement: 38

Armament:

4x 47mm guns

3x 45cm torpedo tubes

1x machine gun (added in 1915)

Tb74 T Class

Tb74-81 T

These boats were designed following an order to develop a coastal torpedo boat, but were classified as sea-going boats. Despite suffering problems with their machinery, they all saw active service and survived the war. The boats were allocated to Romania and Yugoslavia after the war.

Displacement: 262 tonnes

Dimensions: 57.8m x 5.8m x 1.5m

Machinery: Two turbines, 5,000 shp

Speed: 28 knots

Complement: 41

Armament:

2x 66mm guns

2x 45cm torpedo tubes

1x machine gun

Tb82 F Class

Tb82-97 F

Originally only four boats were ordered, but the order was increased when the price was reduced. All the boats of the class saw active service and survived the war. After the war, some were allocated to Romania and Yugoslavia, while others were sold to Portugal and Greece.

Displacement: 244 tonnes

Dimensions: 58.8m x 5.8m x 1.5m

Machinery: Two turbines, 5,000 shp

Speed: 28 knots

Complement: 41

Armament:

2x 66mm guns

2x twin 45cm torpedo tubes

1x machine gun

Tb98 M Class

Tb98-100 M

Commissioned in 1915-1916, all three boats saw active service during the war, and were sold to Greece in 1920.

Displacement: 250 tonnes

Dimensions: 60.4m x 5.6m x 1.5m

Machinery: Two turbines, 5,000 shp

Speed: 29.5 knots

Complement: 41

Armament:

2x 66mm guns

2x twin 45cm torpedo tubes

1x machine gun

Submarines

Before the war, Austria-Hungary purchased six submarines, two each of three different designs. The intention was to evaluate the three designs and use the knowledge gained to determine what was required of an Austro-Hungarian vessel. When war broke out in 1914, these six boats made up the Austro-Hungarian submarine force. Five more submarines had been ordered from Germany, but the order was cancelled (see the U7-class entry).

When war broke out, immediate steps were taken to build up the submarine force, following the cancellation of the order for the five German submarines. U12 was bought and commissioned, and four boats were ordered from Whitehead (the U20 class). In late 1914, the French submarine *Curie* was raised and commissioned as U14 (the number 13 was not used for superstitious reasons), and in 1915 the strength of the submarine force was further increased with the purchase of German UB-type submarines (the U10 class).

After the Allied landings at the Dardanelles, German submarines started to operate in the Adriatic. These submarines kept their German crews, but were temporarily commissioned into the Austro-Hungarian navy, given Austro-Hungarian numbers and flew the Austro-Hungarian flag. This was initially done because Italy had declared war on Austria-Hungary but not Germany, but the practice was continued for some time after the declaration of war between Germany and Italy.

U1 Class

U1, U2

Both members of this class were launched in 1909, and served as training boats during the war. They were declared obsolete in January 1918. Both were handed over to Italy as war reparations in 1920 and scrapped at Pola.

Displacement surfaced: 230 tonnes

Displacement submerged: 249 tonnes

Dimensions: 30.5m x 4.8m x 3.9m

Machinery: Two petrol engines & two electric motors

Speed surfaced: 10.3 knots

Speed submerged: 6 knots

Range surfaced: 950 NM at 6 knots

Range submerged: 40 NM at 2 knots

Complement: 17

Armament:

3x 45cm torpedo tubes (two bow, one stern) with five torpedoes

1x machine gun

U3 Class

U3, U4

U3 and U4 were launched in 1908 in Germany, and towed to Pola via Gibraltar. They suffered continual problems with the diving planes, but had better sea-keeping qualities and living conditions than the other Austro-Hungarian submarines available at the start of the war.

U3 was sunk by the French destroyer *Bisson* in August 1915, after an unsuccessful attack. U4 sank the Italian armoured cruiser *Guiseppe Garibaldi* in July 1915 and survived the war. U4 went to France as a war reparation and was scrapped in 1920.

Displacement surfaced: 240 tonnes

Displacement submerged: 300 tonnes

Dimensions: 42.3m x 4.5m x 3.8m

Machinery: Two kerosene engines & two electric motors

Speed surfaced: 12 knots

Speed submerged: 8.5 knots

Range surfaced: 1,200 NM at 12 knots

Range submerged: 40 NM at 3 knots

Complement: 21

Armament:

2x 45cm torpedo tubes (two bow) with three torpedoes

U5 Class

U5, U6, U12

U5

U5 and U6 were partially built in the United States in 1909 and completed at Whitehead. U12 was built by Whitehead in 1911 and offered to the Austro-Hungarian navy. She was initially refused, but later purchased, and commissioned in August 1914.

U5 was sunk by a mine in May 1917, but raised and rebuilt, with a 75mm gun added. She was ceded to Italy as a war reparation and scrapped in 1920. U6 became the only submarine to be caught by the Otranto Barrage in May 1916, when she became trapped in indicator nets and had to be scuttled. U12 was sunk by a mine in August 1916, then raised by Italy and scrapped.

Displacement surfaced: 240 tonnes

Displacement submerged: 273 tonnes

Dimensions: 32.1m x 4.2m x 3.9m

Machinery: Two petrol engines & two electric motors

Speed surfaced: 10.8 knots

Speed submerged: 8.5 knots

Range surfaced: 800 NM at 8.5 knots

Range submerged: 48 NM at 6 knots

Complement: 19

Armament:

2x 45cm torpedo tubes (two bow) with four torpedoes

1x 75mm gun (U5 only, fitted in 1917)

U7 Class

Five submarines were ordered from Germany to become the U7 class, but were never delivered. When war broke out they were sold back to Germany, as transit through the Strait of Gibraltar was considered too dangerous. They were redesigned to German standards and commissioned into the German navy as U66-70.

Displacement surfaced: 695 tonnes

Displacement submerged: 885 tonnes

Dimensions: 69.5m x 6.3m x 3.9m

Machinery: Two diesel engines & two electric motors

Speed surfaced: 17 knots

Speed submerged: 11 knots

Range surfaced: 6,500 NM at 8 knots

Range submerged: 115 NM at 5 knots

Complement: 36

Armament:

5x 45cm torpedo tubes (four bow, one stern) with nine torpedoes

U10 Class

U10, U11, U15, U16, U17

U10

These were German UB-type submarines, built in Germany and transported via railway to Austria, where they were completed at Pola. U10 and U11 were initially operated by German crews, with an Austro-Hungarian officer aboard each, then later handed over to the Austro-Hungarian navy. U15, U16 and U17 were operated solely by Austro-Hungarian crews.

In October 1916 all boats of the class other than U11 were given 37mm quick-firing deck guns, and U11 was fitted with a 66mm gun. In November 1917 the 37mm guns were replaced with 47mm quick-firing guns.

U16 was scuttled after suffering heavy damage during an attack in which she sank an Italian destroyer. U10 was damaged by a mine in 1918, and towed to Trieste for repair. All surviving members of the class were handed over to Italy as war reparations and scrapped in 1920.

Displacement surfaced: 126 tonnes

Displacement submerged: 140 tonnes

Dimensions: 27.9m x 5.2m x 2.7m

Machinery: One diesel engine & one electric motor

Speed surfaced: 6.5 knots

Speed submerged: 5.5 knots

Range surfaced: 1,500 NM at 5 knots

Range submerged: 45 NM at 4 knots

Complement: 17

Armament:

2x 45cm torpedo tubes (two bow) with two torpedoes

1x 37mm quick-firing gun (fitted in 1916, not U11)

1x 47mm quick-firing gun (replaced 37mm quick-firing gun in 1917, not U11)

1x 66mm gun (fitted in 1916, U11 only)

U14 Class

U14

In December 1914 the French submarine *Curie* was sunk in Pola harbour. She was subsequently raised, refitted and commissioned into the Austro-Hungarian navy as U14. In 1916 she was given new engines and an 88mm gun.

Displacement surfaced: 397 tonnes

Displacement submerged: 551 tonnes

Dimensions: 52.2m x 5.2m x 3.2m

Machinery: Two diesel engines & two electric motors

Speed surfaced: 12.2 knots

Speed submerged: 9 knots

Range surfaced: 1,700 NM at 10 knots

Range submerged: 84 NM at 5 knots

Complement: 28

Armament:

1x 53.3cm torpedo tube (one bow) with one torpedo

6x external 53.3cm torpedo launchers with six torpedoes

1x 47mm gun (later one 88mm gun)

U20 Class

U20, U21, U22, U23

When war broke out the Austro-Hungarian navy ordered four submarines from Whitehead, to be built to the same specification as had been built at the Fiume yard for the Royal Danish Navy prior to the war. Although the navy felt the design had some limitations, more submarines were urgently needed, and so the shortcomings were accepted in order to quickly increase the size of the submarine force. Construction was split between Austrian and Hungarian yards. Problems with construction meant that they were not commissioned until 1917.

U20 and U23 were sunk during the war. U21 and U22 were ceded as war reparations to Italy and France.

Displacement surfaced: 173 tonnes

Displacement submerged: 210 tonnes

Dimensions: 38.8m x 4m x 2.8m

Machinery: One diesel engine & one electric motor

Speed surfaced: 12 knots

Speed submerged: 9 knots

Complement: 18

Armament:

2x 45cm torpedo tubes (two bow) with two torpedoes

1x 66mm gun

1x machine gun

U27 Class

U27, U28, U29, U30, U31, U32, U40, U41

These were licence-built variants of the German UBII type. Ordered in 1915, they were built at Pola and Fiume. They were commissioned in 1917 and 1918. U30 sank in the Otranto Straits. U31 and U41 were ceded to France, the others to Italy, as war reparations.

Displacement surfaced: 264 tonnes

Displacement submerged: 301 tonnes

Dimensions: 36.9m x 4.4m x 3.7m

Machinery: Two diesel engines & two electric motors

Speed surfaced: 9 knots

Speed submerged: 7.5 knots

Complement: 23

Armament:

2x 45cm torpedo tubes (two bow) with four torpedoes

1x 75mm gun

1x machine gun

U43 Class

U43, U47

Built in Germany and transferred by railway, then commissioned as German U-boats. After a year, they were sold to Austria-Hungary and commissioned as U43 and U47.

Both were ceded to France as war reparations

Displacement surfaced: 263 tonnes

Displacement submerged: 292 tonnes

Dimensions: 36.1m x 4.4m x 3.7m

Machinery: Two diesel engines & two electric motors

Speed surfaced: 9.2 knots

Speed submerged: 5.8 knots

Complement: 22

Armament:

2x 50cm torpedo tubes (two bow) with four torpedoes

1x 88mm gun

1x machine gun

U48 Class

U48, U49, U58, U59

A German design, U48 and U49 were laid down but never completed. U58 and U59 were never laid down.

Displacement surfaced: 818 tonnes

Displacement submerged: 1,184 tonnes

Dimensions: 73.3m x 6.7m x 3.3m

Machinery: Two diesel engines & two electric motors

Speed surfaced: 16.3 knots

Speed submerged: 8.5 knots

Complement: 32

Armament:

6x 45cm torpedo tubes (four bow, two stern) with nine torpedoes

2x 9cm guns (U48, U49)

2x 12cm guns (U58, U59)

U50 Class

U50, U51, U56, U57

Licence-built at Fiume, U50 and U51 were laid down but not completed. U56 and U57 were never laid down.

Displacement surfaced: 840 tonnes

Displacement submerged: 1,100 tonnes

Dimensions: 73.5m x 6.3m x 4m

Machinery: Two diesel engines & two electric motors

Speed surfaced: 16.5 knots

Speed submerged: 9 knots

Complement: 33

Armament:

6x 45cm torpedo tubes (four bow, two stern) with nine torpedoes

2x 9cm guns (U50, U51)

2x 12cm guns (U56, U57)

U52 Class

U52, U53, U54, U55

The winner of a competition, U52 and U53 were laid down but not completed. U54 and U55 were never laid down.

Displacement surfaced: 849 tonnes

Displacement submerged: 1,200 tonnes

Dimensions: 76m x 7m x 3.5m

Machinery: Two diesel engines & two electric motors

Speed surfaced: 15.8 knots

Speed submerged: 9 knots

Complement: 40

Armament:

6x 45cm torpedo tubes (four bow, two stern) with nine torpedoes

2x 10cm guns (U52, U53)

2x 12cm guns (U54, U55)

1x machine gun

U101 Class

U101, U102, U103, U104, U105, U106, U118, U119, U120

U101, U102, and U103 were laid down in 1917 and 1918; the other boats were never laid down.

Displacement surfaced: 428 tonnes

Displacement submerged: 620 tonnes

Dimensions: 53.5m x 5.8m x 3.6m

Machinery: Two diesel engines & two electric motors

Speed surfaced: 13.3 knots

Speed submerged: 8.3 knots

Complement: 26

Armament:

5x 45cm torpedo tubes (four bow, one stern) with ten torpedoes

1x 10cm gun

1x machine gun

U107 Class

U107-U141

U107 and U108 were laid down in 1918, but were only around one-third complete by the end of the war. Consequently, not many details of their performance are known.

Displacement surfaced: 791 tonnes

Displacement submerged: 933 tonnes

Dimensions: 69.5m x 7m x unknown

Machinery: Two diesel engines & two electric motors

Complement: 36

Armament:

5x 45cm torpedo tubes (four bow, one stern) with 12 torpedoes

1x 10cm gun

Depot Ships

Gäa

Gäa was built to satisfy a requirement for a fast ship that could follow torpedo ships into battle to refuel and replenish them, as well as being able to defend herself and her charges. In order to save money, she was converted from a Russian auxiliary cruiser. The Russians had themselves converted her from her original role as a German liner. *Gäa* carried 81 torpedoes and 100 mines.

Displacement: 12,310 tonnes

Dimensions: 153.2m x 17.6m x 7.6m

Machinery: Nine boilers, 14,743 ihp

Speed: 18.7 knots

Armament:

4x 12cm L/35 guns

4x 66mm L/44 guns

Lussin

Displacement: 1,000 tonnes

Machinery: Diesel motors, 1,800 hp

Speed: 14 knots

Complement: 154

Armament:

4x 3 pounder

Pelikan

Displacement: 2,430 tonnes

Machinery: 4,000 hp

Speed: 14 knots

Complement: 196

Armament:

2x 9 pounder

8x 3 pounder

Carries 30 torpedoes

Gigant

Displacement: 260 tonnes

Machinery: 400 hp

Speed: 11 knots

Minelayers

Chamaeleon

Launched in 1913, she was the most modern minelayer in the fleet. She survived the war, was ceded to Great Britain, and sold for scrap.

Displacement: 1,100 tonnes

Dimensions: 87.1m x 9.2m x 2.7m

Machinery: Four boilers, 5,500 ihp

Speed: 20.8 knots

Complement: 154

Armament:

2x 90mm L/45 quick-firing guns

2x 90mm L/45 AA guns

300x C-12-type mines

Basilisk

Displacement: 314 tonnes

Speed: 11 knots

Complement: 40

Armament:

2x 3 pounder guns

4x machine guns

150 mines

Carniol

Displacement: 2,812 tonnes

Armament:

200 mines

Salamander

Displacement: 268 tonnes

Speed: 10 knots

Complement: 20

Armament:

2x 3 pounder guns

90 mines

Dromedar

Displacement: 175 tonnes

Speed: 10 knots

Complement: 20

Armament:

3x 3 pounder guns

50 mines

Local Defence Ships

Kronprinz Erzherzog Rudolf

Displacement: 6,900 tonnes

Speed: 16 knots

Complement: 454

Armour:

Belt 300mm steel

Armament:

3x 30cm guns

6x 12cm guns

12x 11 pounder guns

Mars

Launched in 1878 as *Tegetthoff*, she was also used as a training ship.

Displacement: 7,390 tonnes

Speed: 16 knots

Complement: 574

Armour:

Belt 370mm iron

Armament:

6x 24cm guns

5x 15cm guns

2x 11 pounder guns

Yachts

Lakroma

Launched as the light cruiser *Tiger* in 1887, she was renamed and converted to an admiralty yacht in 1905.

Displacement: 1,657 tonnes

Machinery: 6,000 hp

Speed: 18 knots

Complement: 177

Armament:

6x 3 pounder guns

Lussin

Launched in 1883 as a torpedo ship, she was converted into an admiralty yacht in 1910, then became an accommodation ship in 1916.

Machinery: 2 MAN diesels, 1,800 bhp

Speed: 14 knots

Miramar

A paddle wheel steamer, launched in 1872, and used as an imperial yacht.

Displacement: 1,830 tonnes

Machinery: 2,000 hp

Speed: 17 knots

Complement: 159

Armament:

2x 3 pounder guns

2x 1 pounder guns

Dalmat

Launched in 1896

Displacement: 260 tonnes

Machinery: 325 hp

Speed: 12 knots

Other Vessels

Minesweepers

Before the war, torpedo boat numbers 19-27 and 29-40 were converted for use as minesweepers. Requisitioned craft were also used in this role.

Versuchsgleitboot Air-Cushion Boat

This experimental air-cushion boat was based on a private proposal for a hovercraft. The two torpedoes were launched over the stern. It was launched in 1915 and underwent extensive trials, but was eventually cannibalised and scrapped.

Displacement: 7.6 tonnes

Dimensions: 13m x 4m x 0.4m

Machinery: Three petrol engines (one for hovering), 480 bhp

Speed: 32.3 knots

Range: 120 NM

Armament:

2x 45cm torpedoes

1x 8mm machine gun

3x depth charges (added later)

Mb 107 Class Motor Torpedo Boats

Mb 107 - 115

Ordered in December 1916, only three were launched, all in 1918.

Displacement: 26.0 tonnes

Dimensions: 24.6m x 4.6m x 0.6m

Machinery: Three petrol engines, 600 bhp

Speed: 24 knots

Complement: 12

Armament:

1x 66mm L/45 AA gun

2x 8mm machine guns

2x 45cm torpedo tubes

Gleitboot No I Motor Gunboat

The first of two trial hydroplanes, built as a gunboat. The 66mm gun listed below was not fitted when she was put into service in September 1918.

Displacement: 6.7 tonnes

Dimensions: 13.5m x 2.9m x 0.4m

Machinery: Four petrol engines, 600 bhp

Speed: 33.8 knots

Range: 200 NM

Complement: 7

Armament:

1x 66mm L/18 gun (never fitted)

4x 8mm machine guns

4x depth charges

Gleitboot No II Motor Torpedo Boat

The second of two trial hydroplanes, built as a torpedo boat. She seems to have been launched in September 1918 but never completed.

Displacement: 6.7 tonnes

Dimensions: 13.5m x 2.9m x 0.4m

Machinery: Four petrol engines, 600 bhp

Speed: 33.8 knots

Range: 200 NM

Complement: 7

Armament:

1x 35cm torpedo tube

4x 8mm machine guns

Mb 164 Class Assault Craft

Mb 164, Mb 165

Construction started in 1918, inspired by an Italian boat which was captured trying to enter Pola. Mb 164 carried out a test run in October 1918, but was not ready for delivery to Pola before the war ended.

Displacement: 10.5 tonnes

Dimensions: 13.3m x 2.4m x 0.9m

Machinery: Two electric engines, 13 shp

Complement: 3

Armament:

2x 45cm torpedoes

German LM Type Motor Torpedo Boats

LM 3-6, LM 11, LM 12, LM 13

In 1918, it was agreed that six motor torpedo boats intended for the German commander-in-chief of Mediterranean submarines would instead be sold to the Austro-Hungarian navy. LM 13 was not one of these six, but was to be bought once she was completed. The war ended before any of them could reach Pola.

Barsch River Patrol Craft

Launched in 1915, commissioned in 1916. She was handed over to the navy of the Kingdom of Serbs, Croats, and Slovenes in 1919.

Displacement: 129 tonnes

Dimensions: 44m x 6m x 1m

Machinery: 2 boilers, 1,100 shp

Speed: 18 knots

Complement: 42

Armour:

Belt 7.5mm

Deck 6mm

Conning Tower 10mm

Turrets 10mm

Armament:

4x 70mm L/26 guns

3x machine guns

Pola Class Colliers

Pola, Teodo

Launched in 1914 (*Pola*) and 1915 (*Teodo*). Each carried 7,000 tonnes of coal as cargo.

Displacement: 13,200 tonnes

Dimensions: 131m x 17.4m x 7.7m

Machinery: 6,200 hp

Speed: 14 knots

Vesta Oil Tanker

Displacement: 2,130 tonnes

Machinery: 1,200 hp

Speed: 10 knots

Cyclop Repair Ship

Displacement: 2,150 tonnes

Speed: 11 knots

Complement: 93

Armament:

2x 11 pounder guns

Vulkan Repair Ship

Launched in 1877 as a harbour defence ship and named *Prinz Eugen*. She was later converted to a repair ship and renamed *Vulkan*.

Displacement: 3,548 tonnes

Zara Class Training Ships

Zara, Spalato, Sebenico

Launched in 1879 and 1882 as torpedo ships, all three were being used as training vessels by 1914

Displacement: 838 tonnes

Dimensions: 62.7m x 8.2m x 3.7m

Machinery: 2,600 ihp

Speed: 14.3 knots

Tb18 Training Ship

Built as a torpedo boat, she was never fully operational in this role. She served as a training ship during the war.

Displacement: 166 tonnes

Dimensions: 47.3m x 5.3m x 2.8m

Machinery: 2,200 ihp

Speed: 24 knots

Range: 21 NM

Armament:

2x 47mm quick-firing guns

3x torpedo tubes

Herkules Salvage Ship

Displacement: 1,500 tonnes

Dimensions: 64m x 10.3m x 4m

Speed: 10 knots

Complement: 81

Taurus

Displacement: 1,300 tonnes

Dimensions: 67.1m x 9.1m x 4m

Machinery: 2,000 hp

Speed: 15 knots

Armament:

2x 3 pounder guns

2x 1 pounder guns

Albatros Class

Albatros, Nautilus

Tenders to Mars

Displacement: 570 tonnes

Armament:

1x 11 pounder gun

2x 3 pounder guns

Author's Notes

In some cases, classes were up-gunned or otherwise changed between the time they were initially launched and the start of the war. In such cases, the specifications given are those at the start of the war in 1914. If the specification changed during the war, this is noted. Dimensions are given as length x beam x draught. Displacements given are design displacements in metric tonnes, unless otherwise specified. Various guns were designated 7cm, but were actually 66mm calibre. They are listed as 66mm calibre in this book.

The map of the Adriatic is based on this map: http://commons.wikimedia.org/wiki/File:Adriatic_Sea_ map.png by NormanEinstein, and released under the Creative Commons Attribution-Share Alike 3.0 Unported licence. The modified map is released under the same licence, and may be downloaded from www.russellphillipsbooks.co.uk/downloads

Sources and Further Reading

Kemp, Paul; "Austro-Hungarian Battleships"; ISO Publications; 1991

Moore, John; "Jane's fighting ships of World War I"; Studio Editions; 1990

Gardiner, R. & Gray, R. & Budzbon, P.; "Conway's All the world's fighting ships, 1906-1921"; Conway Maritime Press; 1985

Horthy, Nicholas & Simon, Andrew L (translator); "Admiral Nicholas Horthy: memoirs"; Simon Publications; 2000

Halpern, Paul G.; "The Battle of the Otranto Straits: Controlling the Gateway to the Adriatic in World War I"; Indiana University Press; 2004

The World War I Document Archive; www.gwpda.org

FirstWorldWar.com; www.firstworldwar.com

Phillips, Russ; "The Sinking of the Wien"; SOTCW Journal issue 47 (also available on the author's website)

Phillips, Russ; "Szent István; Hungary's Battleship"; SOTCW Journal issue 46 (also available on the author's website)

Digital Reinforcements:
Free Ebook

To get a free ebook of this title, simply go to www.shilka.co.uk/fib and add it to your cart in the normal manner. Then, at checkout, enter discount code BEING49 to get it free.

The free ebook can be downloaded in several formats: Mobi (for Kindle devices & apps), ePub (for other ereaders & ereader apps), and PDF (for reading on a computer). Ereader apps are available for all computers, tablets and smartphones.

About Russell Phillips

Russell Phillips writes books and articles about military technology and history. His articles have been published in Miniature Wargames, Wargames Illustrated and the Society of Twentieth Century Wargamers' Journal. Some of these articles are available on his website.

To get advance notice of new books, join Russell's mailing list at www.rpbook.co.uk/list. Mailing list members get discounts off all of Russell's books, and you can unsubscribe at any time.

Word of mouth is crucial for any author to succeed. If you enjoyed this book, please consider leaving a review where you downloaded it, or on a site like Goodreads. Even a short review would be very much appreciated.

Also by Russell Phillips

Red Steel: Soviet Tanks and Combat Vehicles of the Cold War

The Bear Marches West: 12 Scenarios for 1980's NATO vs Warsaw Pact Wargames

A Damn Close-Run Thing: A Brief History of the Falklands Conflict

This We'll Defend: The Weapons & Equipment of the U.S. Army

Find Russell Phillips Online

Website: www.rpbook.co.uk

Twitter: @RPBook

Facebook: facebook.com/RussellPhillipsBooks

Google Plus: google.com/+RussellPhillips

E-mail: russell@rpbook.co.uk

Join Russell's mailing list: www.rpbook.co.uk/list

CPSIA information can be obtained at www.ICGtesting.com
Printed in the USA
LVOW05s2346301114

416360LV00018B/678/P